PLAY IT SAFE

In the 1981 World Series, in which the New York Yankees faced the Los Angeles Dodgers, New York outfielder Dave Winfield got the players and fans chuckling. Winfield, who had been dubbed the $26 million man for the contract he had recently signed, went to bat sixteen consecutive times without getting a hit. After he finally managed a weak single, he stood on first base and called for the ball as a souvenir. He was kidding, of course. He was poking fun at himself.

Not all of baseball's jokes and pranks are as harmless. Pitcher Rube Waddell of the Philadelphia A's liked to wrestle alligators, and he once jumped out a hotel window to prove that he could fly. (He couldn't.)

If you're tempted to become a jokester or prankster, don't be like Rube Waddell. Never try anything that's reckless. Some of the stunts described in this book could be hazardous to your health if you tried them. Be like Dave Winfield. Keep it simple; play it safe.

INTRODUCTION

Some people couldn't understand the great outfielder Jim Piersall. When he got on first base, he sometimes acted like an ape, scratching himself and making strange noises. When he hit his one hundredth home run, Piersall ran the bases backward.

Piersall, who played for five teams in the course of his career, liked to scrap with the umpires. One day after he had gotten thrown out of a game for arguing, Piersall went up on the roof of the grandstand and continued to hassle the ump from there. Another time, after a close play at second base, Piersall pulled a water pistol from his pocket and squirted the umpire who had called him safe.

Piersall was different. Piersall was goofy.

Baseball has a name for such oddball players—flakes.

It's been said that the term was first used to describe Jackie Brandt, a rookie outfielder with the St. Louis Cardinals in 1956. Brandt once played twenty-seven holes of golf while the heat soared to 101° F (38° C) before a doubleheader. A teammate once said of Brandt that "things seem to flake off his mind and disappear."

This book spotlights baseball's flakes, its wild and crazy guys. They're players who, intentionally or not, do what's unpredictable. They're unusual. They're quirky, sometimes even weird.

For some players, strange conduct comes naturally. Pitcher Turk Wendell of the New York Mets, who liked to hunt during the off-season, often took the mound wearing a heavy necklace made up of the teeth from animals he had killed.

"Guys say I'm a lunatic, but I don't care," Wendell said. "It gives me a psychological edge."

In many instances, players' antics are thought out. The plotting of Montreal pitcher Ross Grimsley earned him a reputation as the team's prankster. He once turned on four fire extinguishers and sprayed them under the hotel door of teammate Stan Bahnsen. "When Stan opened the door," Grimsley recalled, "everything was covered with white foam, including Stan. It looked like the Alps."

Outfielder John Lowenstein, a valued performer with the Baltimore Orioles during their World Series years of 1979 and 1983, liked to go up to strangers in airports, look at their name tags, shake hands, and say, "Why if it isn't so-and-so; how's the family?" He'd usually end up having a long conversation with the person because they thought they really knew him.

Lowenstein always denied he was flakey. "I just keep myself entertained," he once told *Sport* magazine. "Baseball is reality at its harshest. It's a stress existence. You have to introduce a fictional world to survive."

Other times, wackiness is unplanned; it just happens. Outfielder José Canseco, playing for the Texas Rangers, once eased back on the warning track to catch a fly ball. Before he could get his glove up, the ball fell out of the night sky to plunk Canseco on the top of the head and rebound over the fence for a home run. Canseco's mishap was one of the great bonehead plays of the season.

However it happens, more than a few baseball observers agree that wacky behavior in baseball is on the decline. Many of today's players, it's said, are boring. "There just aren't that many flakey guys anymore," said Jim Hawkins of the *Detroit Free Press*. "They may be a dying breed." Peter Gammons noted in the *Boston Globe* that "the era of colorful baseball has died in Boston."

It may be that the enormous salaries paid players nowadays have made the difference. To a player who is earning something more than a million dollars a year, baseball is not a game—it's big business. He is much less likely to be a clown or a clubhouse prankster. In other words, the free-spirited player is going the way of baggy uniforms and the twenty-five cent hot dog.

Despite the trend, flakiness does persist. There's just less of it today than there used to be.

Flakes, pranksters, and blockheads have a value. They help to keep their teammates relaxed and they play better as a result. They make baseball fun for players and fans alike. It's a shame their number is shrinking. They are to be missed.

FOOD FREAKS

Players are sometimes driven to nonsensical conduct by their superstitions. Often these involve food.

Wade Boggs, for example, made a point to eat chicken before every game he ever played. (Boggs, a bundle of superstitions, also ran wind sprints at exactly 7:17 P.M. before night games and he took exactly one hundred ground balls when warming up.)

Don't laugh! When Boggs retired in 1999 after an eighteen-year career with the Red Sox, Yankees, and Devil Rays, he could lay claim to five American League batting titles and a lifetime average of .328. He also had two Gold Glove awards for his sparkling play at third base.

Jim "Catfish" Hunter, a Hall of Fame pitcher for the Oakland A's and New York Yankees, always included fish in his pregame meal. Flounder was his favorite.

And then there is Mickey Tettleton, whose career as a catcher, first baseman, and outfielder with the Rangers, Tigers, Orioles, and A's covered fourteen seasons. Tettleton attributed his baseball success to dining on Froot Loops.

QUIRKY TURK

Steven John "Turk" Wendell, a leading oddball player of the twenty-first century, liked the number nine. When he was traded to the Mets from the Chicago Cubs in 1997, the New York team issued him uniform No. 10. Wendell asked for No. 9. Someone else had it, he was told.

Wendell then asked for No. 99. No problem. He wore the number throughout his career with the team.

Late in 2000, the thirty-three-year-old Wendell negotiated a new contract with the Mets. The club agreed to pay him $10 million over a three-year period.

No, said Wendell. He didn't want $10 million. He wanted one penny less than that amount.

The Mets agreed. The contract that Wendell negotiated guaranteed him a salary of $9,999,999.99 if he pitched seventy games in each of the next three seasons. With all those nines, Wendell felt confident of success.

Wendell was a key member of the Mets bullpen. A setup man, his job was to hold the lead for Armando Benitez, the New York team's closer. With his solid fastball and sharp-breaking slider, Wendell was looked upon as one of the National League's best eighth-inning pitchers. He was a good fielder and had a reliable move to first base.

But Turk Wendell was much better known for his wacky behavior than anything else. He developed one of his more bizarre habits during his tenure as a pitcher at Quinnipiac College in Hamden, Connecticut. Some of his teammates chewed tobacco. The pranksters among them would sometimes spit tobacco juice on Wendell's shoes.

Wendell couldn't bring himself to chew tobacco so he couldn't spit back. As a substitute, Wendell began chewing licorice. The black candy made it possible for him to give the tobacco chewers a dose of their own medicine. But the licorice stained his teeth. Wendell had a solution. Between innings in the dugout, he brushed his teeth.

Asked about the unusual practice, Wendell shrugged. "I just believe in good dental hygiene," he said.

Wendell continued his antics in the minor leagues. When he pitched for the Iowa Cubs, a farm team of the Chicago Cubs, his play-

fulness made him a favorite of children between the ages of four and fourteen. He signed every autograph. He played catch with them in the parking lot. He took them fishing. Kids loved him.

When he was called up to play for the parent team, however, his clownishness caused more distress than joy. The umpire would always roll the ball to him to start an inning. He had been warned to do so by the catcher. If the umpire threw the ball to Wendell, he wouldn't attempt to catch it. Instead, he would let it hit him on the chest and fall to the ground.

"I like to pick the ball up from the mound to start an inning," Wendell explained.

Before he threw the first pitch of an inning, Wendell always waved to the center fielder. He would then stand and wait for him to wave back. If the center fielder didn't respond, Wendell would wave to the right fielder. If he didn't wave back, he would wave to the left fielder.

Wendell explained that the custom dated to his days as a high school pitcher. His best friend, Jim Duquette, played center field. They always waved to each other before the start of an inning.

Once Wendell got around to pitching, he worked very fast. The batters sometimes stepped out of the box in an attempt to slow Wendell down. Wendell didn't like that. Sometimes he would yell at the umpire to make the batter step up to the plate.

As this suggests, Wendell was very intense as a pitcher. He got charged up.

On the night before a game in which he was set to pitch, Wendell often couldn't sleep. He'd do crossword puzzles or write poems. He also passed the time by painting pictures by numbers. Since Wendell is color-blind, producing a picture in paint in the usual way wasn't possible.

And Wendell wouldn't eat on the days he was to pitch. He'd drink orange juice instead.

During the off-season, Wendell liked to hunt. "I grew up in Dalton, Massachusetts, in the western part of the state, where there's a lot of wilderness," Wendell once told *The Sporting News*. "I used to tag along with my father on hunting expeditions and went out on my own when I was eight years old.

"These days I hunt whenever I can, including trips during the off-season to Alabama, Montana, North Dakota, Pennsylvania, and other places, too."

Wendell said he liked hunting because it brought him "close to nature." He enjoyed "watching nature take its course and being part of it. I can't play baseball forever," said Wendell. "But hopefully I can hunt for as long as I live."

MAD AND MADDER

During the 1970s, he reigned as baseball's most colorful player and a favorite among fans of the St. Louis Cardinals. A relief pitcher with a smoking fastball, his name was Alan Thomas Hrabosky, but everyone knew him as "The Mad Hungarian."

When he was called into a game, Hrabosky would stomp out of the bullpen, his face a mask of hatred. Once he reached the mound, he would turn his back on the plate and work himself into a wild-eyed frenzy.

His shoulders would twitch. His facial muscles would tighten. All the while, he would be muttering to himself. Hrabosky called it "controlled rage." As a final gesture, he would slam the ball into his mitt, then turn and face the hitter.

"I'm getting myself into a concentrated hate mood," Hrabosky said. "I want the hitter to wonder if maybe I *am* a little crazy."

To go with his routine, Hrabosky had a fearful appearance. Stocky, almost 6 feet (183 centimeters) tall, he had slitted eyes and dark brown hair that flowed out from beneath his cap. He also had a thick mustache, the ends of which curled down to his chin in a menacing fashion.

Once Hrabosky was ready to deliver the ball, he would nod to the catcher, spin on his left foot, then kick his right leg toward the plate. He held his glove in front of his face, pulling it away at the last instant to give the hitter a glimpse of the hatred in his eyes.

Almost every pitch he threw was a fastball. "It puts extra fear in the mind of the hitter," he said. "It makes him easier to destroy."

Hrabosky said that he developed his Mad Hungarian routine after studying pitcher Bob Gibson, one of the Cardinals all-time greats. Hrabosky noticed that Gibson always scowled at the hitter. He would challenge him with fastballs high and inside. Gibson made the hitter fear him; he intimidated him.

From Gibson, Hrabosky said, "I learned my first lesson in the major leagues. Be an intimidator."

The terror that Hrabosky dished out helped him compile ninety-seven career saves. And with sixty-five wins against only thirty-four losses, he had one of the best all-time winning percentages for a reliever. He also became one of St. Louis's most beloved athletes.

After he retired in 1982, Hrabosky went on to a career in television, broadcasting Cardinals games. Known for his sharp wit, he also had a popular baseball radio show. He devoted much of his time to local charities, too.

As a broadcaster, Hrabosky preferred to be called Al. "The Mad Hungarian is always going to be a part of me," he said, "but now I don't need him." For St. Louis fans to see Al in his role as the Mad Hungarian, they had to attend Cardinals Old-Timers Games.

STRANGE BIRD

No book that puts the spotlight on baseball's wackiest players would be complete without reporting on the antics of a tall, youthful fireballer with frizzy hair named Mark Steven Fidrych, a rookie pitcher with the Detroit Tigers in 1976. He was fresh. He was funny. He was one of the biggest baseball sensations in years.

The uproar that Fidrych created was wholly unexpected. From Northboro, Massachusetts, the twenty-one-year-old Fidrych wasn't even on the Detroit roster for the first month of the season and he sat almost unnoticed on the Detroit bench.

Fidrych got his first start on May 15, 1976, against the Cleveland Indians. He was outstanding. He had a no-hitter for six innings and went on to win, 2–1, giving up only two hits.

But it wasn't Fidrych's explosive fastball and wicked slider that started people talking. It was the zany things he did on the mound. He would talk to the baseball, holding it in front of his face, telling it where he wanted it to go. He would get down on his hands and knees before an inning and pat the dirt in the mound, smoothing it out to his liking.

Whenever he gave up a hit, he had another bizarre habit. He believed that the hit had tainted the ball. When it was returned to him, he would walk off the mound and lob the ball to the umpire, and ask for a new one.

When an inning was over, Fidrych would sprint back to the dugout. He wanted to be there when his teammates arrived so he could thank them for their good play.

In the way Fidrych stormed about the mound, someone said that he looked like Big Bird on the TV program *Sesame Street*. It wasn't long before he had become known everywhere as Mark "The Bird" Fidrych.

Fidrych turned Detroit upside down. The Tigers were a fifth-place team that season. When he made his pitching debut, he performed in a near-empty park. But when word got out about The Bird, Detroit fans flocked to see him. Thousands bought "Bird" T-shirts and orange-and-black buttons with the phrase, "The Bird is the Word." A couple announced they were naming their newborn after him.

Fidrych appealed to people because he was so natural. He didn't plan his antics in advance. Talking to the ball and speeding to and from the dugout were part of his pitching routine, like looking in for the catcher's signs or covering first base.

Fidrych charmed interviewers with his honesty. He spoke of how he planned to go home to Northboro after the season and pump gas at a local service station. He liked wearing T-shirts and blue jeans. He complained that the Tigers made him wear "good clothes" when the team traveled.

While other players drove expensive cars, Fidrych pulled up to Tiger Stadium in a green subcompact. "I'd like a motorcycle," he said, "but I'd really like to drive a pickup. I'm a truck man."

Fidrych's popularity created problems for the Detroit manager Ralph Houk. Fans of the Tigers demanded to see him perform at Tiger Stadium. Houk had to juggle his pitching assignments so Detroit supporters could see him more. "I'd be a liar if I said I didn't try to pitch him more at home," Houk said.

In one of his appearances, The Bird faced the New York Yankees in a game that was nationally televised. Some 10,000 fans had to be turned away from Tiger Stadium that night. After he had shut down the New York team, 5–1, and hugged his teammates, 50,000 fans refused to leave their seats. They cheered and applauded until The Bird came back on the field for a curtain call. "I've never seen anything like it," said Ralph Houk.

Fidrych was not merely a flake. He was also an exceptional pitcher. He had excellent control. He kept the ball down and moved it around.

"He's not as flakey as they say," Houk declared. "When he's on the mound, he doesn't know that anyone else is around. He talks to himself to help his concentration. As a rule, we play good in the field behind him. Players like to play behind a guy who throws strikes."

By early August, Fidrych boasted a record of eleven wins and only three losses. He had completed all but two of his fifteen starts. His earned run average of 1.80 was the best in the major leagues.

Named to the American League's All-Star team, he was handed the starting assignment, an unusual honor for a rookie. He gave up four hits and the National League's first two runs and ended up as the game's losing pitcher. But overall, it was an extraordinary season for The Bird. He finished with a 19-9 record. His earned run average of 2.34 was the best of all starting pitchers in the major leagues. Nobody was surprised when Fidrych was named Rookie of the Year in the American League.

Mark Fidrych seemed to be on the road to a Hall of Fame career, but it never happened. Plagued by injuries, The Bird won only ten more games for the Tigers from 1977 through 1980. He pitched for a Detroit farm team before the club released him.

He continued to hope that he could make a comeback. A couple of more seasons in the minor leagues convinced him to retire.

In 2001, twenty-five years after his remarkable season, The Bird was interviewed by Michael J. Happy of the *Detroit News*. He was asked if he had memories of all that had happened a quarter of a century before. "It was huge," Fidrych said. "It will never be just a blur to me."

In 1976, Fidrych earned $16,500, the league minimum at the time. He was asked whether he resented the enormous sums that players of the day were receiving.

"It's all relative," said Fidrych. "Times have changed. I thought I made a ton of money in my time."

Kids of the twenty-first century never heard of The Bird, Fidrych was told. How did he feel about that?

"It doesn't bother me," Fidrych said. "Kids are growing up in their own era right now, not looking at the past.

"That's what happens when you get old."

THE MARVELOUS ONE

The 1962 New York Mets were perhaps the most pitiful team in baseball history. Made up of inexperienced youngsters and castoffs from other teams, the Mets lost the first nine games they played that season. A few weeks later, they embarked on another losing streak, one that reached seventeen games.

"They've shown me ways to lose I never thought existed," said manager Casey Stengel. The hapless Mets ended up losing 120 games that season, the all-time record.

The Mets sorry play came to be symbolized by first baseman Marv Throneberry. A balding veteran, Throneberry had trouble fielding ground balls and handling throws. Every pop-up was an adventure for him.

Although the fans often booed poor Marv, they took pity on him and his blunders. Marvelous Marv, they called him.

In a typical game late in his career, Marv fumbled a ground ball and the error allowed a run to score. When he came to bat in the bottom half of the inning, Marv wore a serious look. In the batter's box, he took several potent practice swings. It was obvious that he wanted to make up for his misplay.

On the first pitch, Marv lifted a towering fly between outfielders. As the ball rolled toward the wall, Marv rounded first, lumbered past second, and went sliding into third for a triple. Marv's fans stood and cheered.

But the play wasn't over. The opposing team claimed that Marv had failed to touch second base. The umpire agreed. Marv was called out.

Manager Stengel stormed out of the dugout to protest. But before he had a chance to present his case to the umpire, the team's first base coach stopped him. "Don't bother, Casey," said the coach. "He didn't touch first, either."

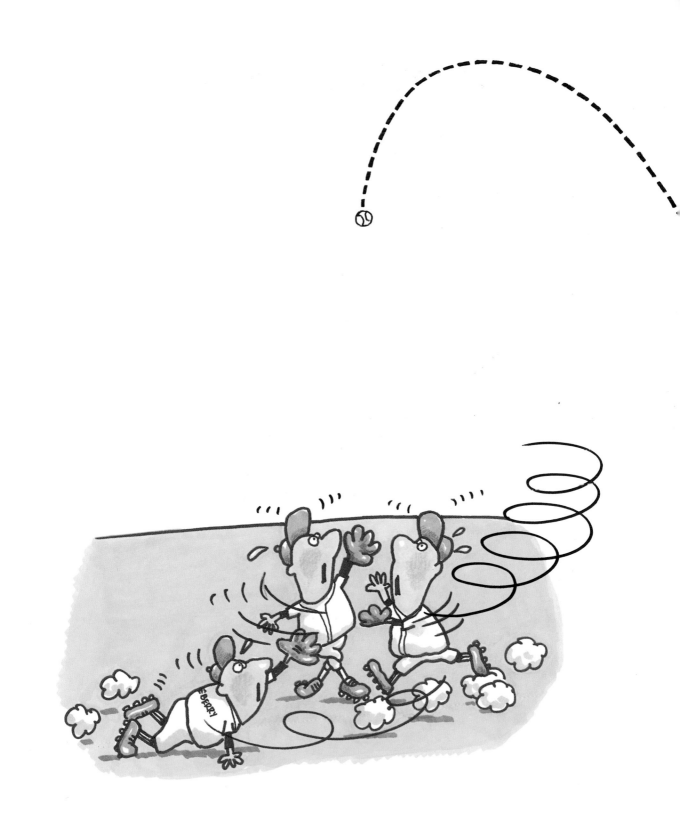

FUNNYMAN

Catcher Bob Uecker batted over .300 three times when he played for Louisville in the American Association. But after he arrived in the National League with Milwaukee in 1962, Uecker's bat turned feeble, and it stayed that way. Nevertheless, Uecker managed to endure in the major leagues for six seasons, getting by on his defensive skills and a rifle arm.

While Uecker was never much more than a so-so player, he was an All-Star when it came to joke-telling and making people laugh. He later enjoyed a long career as a broadcaster of Brewers games.

Uecker's lifetime batting average of exactly .200 was often the subject of his humor. In a late-night talk show, Uecker once noted, "Most people's bats said 'Powerized' down at the end. Mine said 'For Display Purposes Only.'"

Not being very fast on the base paths was another of Uecker's failings. "I lacked speed," Uecker admitted. "I had to compensate with a few tricks. One was to knock my hat off as I ran down the first baseline to make it appear that I was really moving."

Here are other examples of Uecker's wit:

- "Anybody with ability can play in the big leagues. But to be able to trick people year in and year out the way I did, I think that was a much greater feat."

- "I had slumps that lasted into the winter."

- "Sporting goods companies pay me not to endorse their products."

- "I remember one time I'm batting against the Dodgers in Milwaukee. They lead, 2–1, it's the bottom of the ninth, bases loaded, two out and the pitcher has a full count on me. I look over to the Dodgers dugout and they're all in their street clothes."

- "I knew when my career was over. In 1965 my baseball card came out with no picture."

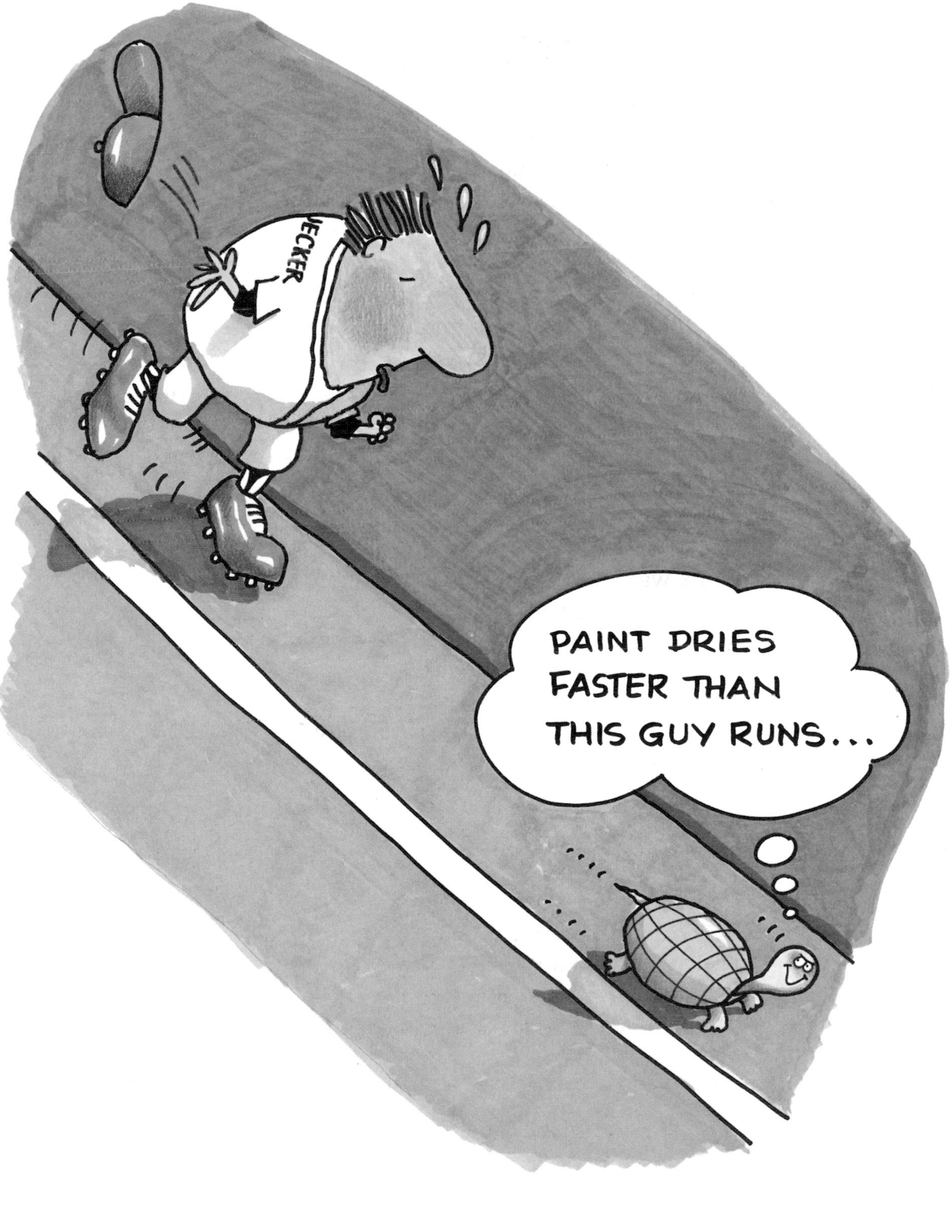
UECKER
PAINT DRIES FASTER THAN THIS GUY RUNS...

PUT TO SHAME

Rick Honeycutt, a left-handed pitcher from Chattanooga, Tennessee, had a twenty-one-year major-league career with six different teams. It was a career that had more ups and downs than a roller-coaster ride.

A control pitcher, Honeycutt was a rookie with the Seattle Mariners in 1977. After being traded to the Texas Rangers in 1981, he endured several mediocre seasons before winning Comeback Player of the Year honors in 1983. With the Oakland A's in 1988, he won games in the League Championship Series and World Series. Those were some of the highs.

A notable low point in his career came on September 30, 1980. Pitching for the Mariners, Honeycutt faced the Kansas City Royals in Seattle's Kingdome. Royals players noticed that Honeycutt's pitches were acting in a wild and crazy manner, veering this way and that as they crossed the plate.

Willie Wilson, an outfielder for the Royals, suspected that Honeycutt was tampering with the ball in some manner. After Wilson tripled, he watched Honeycutt carefully from his perch on third base.

George Brett came to the plate for the Royals and singled, sending Wilson home. Wilson then asked plate umpire Bill Kunkel to check the ball, Honeycutt's glove, and his glove hand.

The game was halted while Kunkel went to the mound and began his inspection. It didn't take the umpire long to discover tape on the index finger of Honeycutt's right hand with a thumbtack stuck up through the tape. In addition, a small piece of sandpaper was attached to the tape.

Honeycutt was thought to be using the tack and sandpaper to scuff up the surface of the ball to get a better grip on it. Kunkel immediately tossed Honeycutt out of the game.

As the thoroughly humiliated Honeycutt trudged toward the dugout, he reached up to wipe his forehead. He forgot the tack was still taped to his finger and left a bright red scratch across his brow.

In the locker room, Honeycutt, who was later suspended for ten days, was filled with regret. "I haven't been in trouble like that since the last time I was sent to the principal's office," he said.

"What an ordeal," he added. "Crime never pays."

OUT OF THIS WORLD

In a major-league career that stretched from the late 1960s to the mid 1980s, outfielder Jay Johnstone played for no fewer than eight major-league teams. On each, he was the head clown and chief practical joker.

A rundown of all of Johnstone's spoofs and stunts would require a book much longer than this one. He once lit a firecracker under a broadcaster's feet as he was interviewing a player on television. When it rained, Johnstone would sometimes put on an umbrella hat.

"Lots of people think I'm crazy, from another world," Johnstone said. "But that doesn't bother me. Baseball is a business, but you have to have fun. It makes it easier to win when you do that."

After Johnstone was traded to the Los Angeles Dodgers in 1980, Tommy Lasorda, a Dodgers coach at the time, told him that the club-house was too quiet. "He told me he wanted me to change all that," Johnstone once recalled. "He said he wanted me to loosen guys up, make the ballpark a fun place for them to be."

Johnstone didn't have to be told twice. One of the first things he did was buy spray cans of green paint. He began secretly spraying green on players' bats and shoes. When a victim griped, Johnstone would grin and say it was the work of the Green Hornet. He began sneaking into players' hotel rooms to spray big green GHs on walls and ceilings.

Johnstone got several of his teammates to join him in his scheme, including pitcher Jerry Reuss and first baseman Steve Garvey. Coach Lasorda was a frequent target of Johnstone and his buddies. They once spray painted a GH on Lasorda's bedsheets, although they risked having to pay for the damage. "I know you're the Green Hornet," Lasorda once told Johnstone. "I just can't prove it."

Johnstone pulled off one of his most memorable tricks during spring training in Florida in 1981. The Dodgers were scheduled to leave on a three-hour bus trip from Vero Beach, where the team had its head-quarters, to Orlando. There the Dodgers were scheduled to play an exhibition game against the Minnesota Twins. The bus was due to depart at 7:30 A.M. That meant that Lasorda would have to get up around six o'clock in order to have breakfast.

"Tommy has never met a meal he hasn't liked," Johnstone noted. "He wasn't about to skip breakfast."

The night before, Johnstone got a master key and slipped into Lasorda's room and removed parts from Lasorda's telephone. He knew that Lasorda always left a wake-up call with the hotel switchboard. But now the message would never get through because of Johnstone's tampering.

The next morning, Lasorda became furious when he woke up, glanced at the clock, and found that he had overslept by almost an hour. Unless he hurried, he knew he would miss breakfast. He quickly showered and dressed. But when he tried to leave his room, the door wouldn't open. Johnstone had tied a rope from the knob, through a hallway window, to a big palm tree outside. Johnstone didn't seem to mind that what he had done was very dangerous, a threat to Lasorda's well-being.

Lasorda rushed to the telephone to call the front desk. The phone was dead.

Lasorda went berserk. Dodger pitcher Steve Howe, in a room next to Lasorda's, heard him shout a stream of unprintable words. Ted

Power, another Dodger pitcher, was awakened by Lasorda's screams. Power was sleeping two rooms away.

A hotel employee finally heard Lasorda and let him out of his room. The fuming Lasorda managed to get to the team bus before it left but he missed breakfast.

On the bus, Lasorda spotted Johnstone. "Just stay away from me today!" Lasorda shouted. "Just keep out of my sight!"

Johnstone did.

SPECIAL DAYS

Relief pitcher John Franco, who had a long and illustrious career with the New York Mets, isn't likely to forget Saturday, May 12, 1996. It was John Franco Day. Before the game, a ceremony was held at home plate to honor the gritty Franco for recording his three hundredth save.

Afterward, the Mets faced the Chicago Cubs. In the bottom of the first inning, Chicago pitcher Kevin Foster fired an inside fastball that headed straight for Todd Hundley's head. Hundley ducked just in time and escaped injury. To pay back the Cubs, Mets pitcher Pete Harnisch drilled Foster with a fastball in the second inning.

The bad feelings erupted into a full-scale brawl in the fifth inning, with both benches emptying. The umpires ejected nine players for fighting. Franco was one of them.

When Franco was needed in the ninth inning to quell a Chicago rally, he was unable to answer the call. The hero of the day sat in the clubhouse with a cut beneath his eye, watching the game on television.

Another similar reversal of fortune took place on September 30, 1992. That was the day slugger George Brett rapped out his three thousandth hit. It took Brett only a few seconds to turn the cheers into boos by getting picked off of first base.

CON MAN

Dave Bresnahan, a catcher with the Eastern League's Williamsport Bills, never made it to the major leagues. And his career in the minors was very brief. But Bresnahan earned lasting fame as a prize flake for a play he tried to pull off during the 1987 season.

The Bills were playing the Reading Phillies, who had a runner on third base. Bresnahan threw to third base in an attempt to pick off the runner.

But Bresnahan did not throw the ball. That was still in his glove. What he had thrown was a peeled potato. It was round like a baseball. It was white. Everyone thought it was a ball.

Bresnahan's throw was high. It sailed over the third baseman's glove. The runner took off for home.

Imagine his surprise when he saw Bresnahan waiting for him, ball in hand. The umpire called the runner out.

There was chaos after that. The Phillies protested. Bresnahan's manager removed him from the game and fined him $50. He was released by Williamsport the next day.

The potato? It ended up in three pieces in the outfield. Too bad. It should have gone to the Hall of Fame.

IN REVERSE

Herman "Germany" Schaefer was never any better than mediocre as a hitter, but thanks to his versatility as a fielder he managed to stay in the majors for thirteen seasons. Although normally a second baseman, Schaefer played every infield and outfield position, and once, while with the Washington Senators in 1914, even pitched.

What Schaefer is more famous for, however, is his zany base running. He is the only player known to have stolen *first* base.

Schaefer was an infielder for the Detroit Tigers at the time the unlikely incident took place. The team was playing the Cleveland Indians. The Tigers had Davy Jones on third base. Schaefer was at first. The score was tied.

To get in the tie-breaking run, a delayed double steal was called. Schaefer was to attempt a theft of second. When catcher Nig Clarke threw to second in an effort to nail Schaefer, Jones was to take off for home plate.

Schaefer went sliding into second to execute the first part of the play. But catcher Clarke held the ball, making no attempt to get Schaefer.

Schaefer, upset that the team's strategy hadn't worked, raced back to first base on the next pitch. Then he shouted across the diamond to Davy Jones, still perched on third, telling him that he was going to steal second base again.

The pitcher pumped and delivered. Schaefer, true to his word, hustled to second base. The catcher, thoroughly rattled by Schaefer's antics, threw to second. When he did, Jones hurried home with the go-ahead run.

The fact that Schaefer had stolen first base disturbed baseball officials. When the season ended, they changed the rules. They made it mandatory that base runners, like racehorses and stock cars, travel only in a counterclockwise direction. The change assured that Germany Schaefer would remain as the only ballplayer to have stolen first base.

TRICKSTER

Practical joking has a rich history in baseball, going back to the days when players rode trains from one city to another and the grass was always real. For every team, there's a long list of players who seemed to thrive on getting teammates into uncomfortable situations.

Some practical jokes are well known. The hotfoot, for instance. Putting knots in a player's clothing or nailing a teammate's shoes to the floor have also been popular through the years.

In recent years, however, such tricks have been cast aside in favor of more creative efforts. Today's practical jokers often employ careful thought and planning.

Take Jim Rooker, for instance. A red-haired left-hander for the Pittsburgh Pirates during most of the 1970s, Rooker once pulled a stunt that had major-league clubhouses abuzz for weeks. It was both original and imaginative.

One day, Rooker got to the ballpark very early, before any of his teammates. He removed all of the bottles of soda and metal shelving from the soft drink cooler in the clubhouse. Then he climbed inside, closing the door behind him.

Unlike most refrigerators, the cooler had openings through which air could enter. Otherwise, Rooker's prank could have ended tragically.

Rooker waited in the icy blackness, his knees drawn up to his chin. Before long, he heard voices and he knew his teammates were beginning to arrive.

Finally, the magic moment arrived. Outfielder John Milner was the victim. Milner opened the refrigerator door and reached in for a Coke or Pepsi. Rooker was ready. He grabbed Milner's hand with his near frozen paws. At the same time, Rooker let out a blood-chilling scream.

Milner snatched his hand free of Rooker's grasp and fell back in shock. The others in the clubhouse had no idea what had happened until they saw Rooker climbing out of the fridge, a wide grin on his face.

Milner was truly unnerved by the incident. Long after, he sat in the corner of the trainer's room, silent and shaken.

SLEIGHT OF HAND

In a game at Yankee Stadium in 1983, George Brett, a notable slugger with the Kansas City Royals, caused a great uproar with his pine tar bat. Pine tar is, of course, the sticky, smelly substance that a hitter applies to the bat handle to improve his grip.

After Brett had socked a home run, Yankees manager Billy Martin complained to the umpire that the pine tar on Brett's bat was not limited to the handle of the bat. It extended up toward the barrel, going well beyond the limit set by the rules. Therefore, the bat was illegal and the homer did not count, Martin claimed. The ump agreed.

Brett went berserk. He came storming out of the dugout to argue with the umpire. It didn't matter; the ruling stuck. The game, which had been halted, was completed, with the Royals winning.

A few days later, however, American League president Lee MacPhail reversed the umpire's ruling. The home run counted, MacPhail said.

The Brett incident wasn't the first time that pine tar made headlines. In a game in Pittsburgh in 1968, pitcher Bob Moose of the Pirates, a strong right-hander, got in trouble for throwing a pine tar *ball*.

The twenty-year-old Moose, a rookie at the time, was facing the league-leading Cardinals. He was no mystery to the St. Louis hitters. They nailed him for four hits and two runs in the second inning.

Back in the dugout as the Pirates batted, Moose happened to notice a teammate in the on-deck circle rubbing down the handle of his bat with a pine tar rag. If that gooey stuff could improve a batter's grip, Moose thought, perhaps it could do the same for a pitcher. Before he went out to the mound for the next inning, Moose rubbed the fingers of his right hand, his pitching hand, with brownish goo.

To say that the pine tar made Moose a better pitcher is to understate what happened. Moose was transformed. His fastball moved like a snake. His breaking pitches dipped and dived. Moose was unhittable. He felt supreme, like a candidate for the Cy Young Award.

Moose's dreams of glory didn't last very long. After a sequence in which he struck out four consecutive St. Louis batters, Cardinals man-

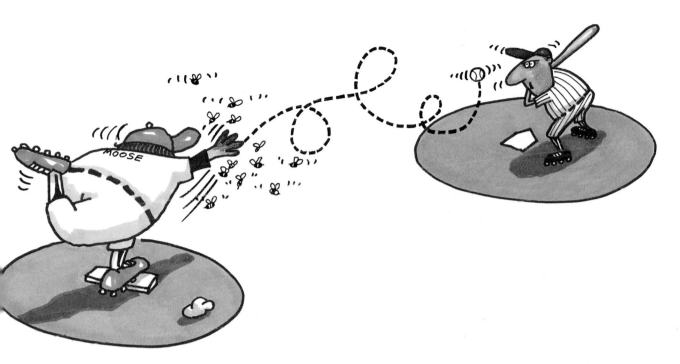

ager Red Schoendienst began to suspect that something was afoot. He called time and went up to the plate umpire Chris Pelekoudas and asked him to examine Moose's right hand.

Pelekoudas went to the mound and began his inspection. He looked carefully at Moose's fingers. They looked like they had been coated with pine tar. He sniffed the fingers. They smelled liked pine tar. It *was* pine tar.

Pelekoudas sent Moose to the clubhouse to wash off the pine tar. When he returned, the umpire examined his fingers again. They were clean.

Once Moose resumed pitching, he was his ordinary self again. He quickly gave up two more runs before being removed from the game for a reliever.

Bob Moose went on to pitch for the Pirates for another nine years. He tossed a no-hitter in 1969. He pitched in the League Championship Series three times. In 1971 he pitched in the World Series. He ended his career with 76 wins in 147 decisions. But never once did he attain the mastery he had that night in 1968 against the Cardinals.

FACE OFF

The Kingsport (Tennessee) Braves in the Appalachian League once boasted a pitcher named Audry Scruggs, a nineteen year old who had the unusual talent of being able to throw equally well with either hand. When a rightie batter came to the plate, Scruggs, to gain a tactical advantage, would throw right-handed. With a leftie hitter at bat, Scruggs became a southpaw.

One day Scruggs faced switch-hitter Dan Spain of the Elizabethton (Tennessee) Twins. Against Scruggs, Spain decided to bat right-handed.

Scruggs got set to deliver the ball with his right hand. Seeing this, Spain hopped over to the left side of the plate. Scruggs shrugged and switched the ball to his left hand. Spain hopped back.

The duel continued. Spain kept jumping from one side of the plate to the other. Scruggs kept changing hands.

The plate umpire finally called a halt to the silliness. He ordered Spain to decide whether he wanted to bat from the right or left side.

Spain chose to be a rightie. Scruggs, pitching from the right side, got him to ground out.

JIM-DANDY

During the 1950s and most of the 1960s, no player brought more craziness to baseball than Jimmy Piersall. In his seventeen-year career with five teams, Piersall was often a colorful sideshow as he clashed with opposing players, teammates, umpires, and fans.

Piersall's wacky behavior often overshadowed the fact that he was an outstanding defensive player and not a bad hitter. He won two Gold Gloves as a center fielder and his .990 lifetime fielding percentage is among the highest of all time. During his career, Piersall hit .272 and 104 home runs.

"He's great, but you have to play him in a cage," said Casey Stengel, Piersall's manager when he played for the New York Mets.

Born in Waterbury, Connecticut, in 1929, Piersall was a standout baseball player at fourteen. He also starred in basketball, leading his high school team to three straight New England championship finals, one of which they won.

After high school, Piersall signed with the Red Sox. Four years in the minor leagues followed before he moved up to the Boston team.

It didn't take very long for Piersall to earn a reputation as a clown. For instance, he liked to call attention to himself by taking a bow after almost every catch.

Sometimes his antics weren't amusing. He stirred up a fight with the Yankees' second baseman Billy Martin. He also tangled with Red Sox teammate Mickey McDermott.

Early in June 1950 during his rookie season in a game against the St. Louis Browns, Piersall grabbed the spotlight. The Browns led, 9–5, as the game entered the bottom half of the ninth inning. Forty-six-year-old Satchel Paige was on the mound for the Browns.

Piersall, the first batter to face Paige in the inning, announced that he was going to bunt. Not only did he do exactly what he said he would do, he beat the throw to first base.

Once at first, Piersall began to mimic Paige's every move. When the tall and lanky right-hander stared in to get the sign, Piersall stared in to get the sign. When Paige wound up, Piersall wound up. When Paige released the ball, Piersall would let out a shrill piggish squeal, so loud that it could be heard in both dugouts.

Paige went to pieces. Six runs poured across the plate and the Red Sox won.

Before the season ended, the high-strung, emotional Piersall suffered a mental breakdown, and entered a hospital for treatment. He was back with the Red Sox in 1953, playing right field. In one game that season, Piersall went 6-for-6, tying an American League record.

Piersall was traded to the Cleveland Indians after the 1958 season. When the Indians visited Boston to play the Red Sox, Piersall unveiled a scheme to defend against Ted Williams, the greatest hitter of the time. When Williams came to bat, Piersall sprinted back and forth across the outfield in an effort to distract him.

The umpires were much more disturbed than Williams was. They signaled that Piersall was to be ejected. Piersall raced from the outfield to argue, slamming his cap and glove to the ground. When Cleveland manager Joe Gordon came to Piersall's defense, he, too, was tossed out.

The uproar had little effect upon Williams. He went 1-for-3, his hit being a home run. The next day, Fenway Park was jammed to the rafters by Boston fans who came to boo Piersall.

Piersall got into three arguments with umpires that afternoon, as the Red Sox swept the Indians in both games of a doubleheader. During a game delay, Piersall hid behind the flagpole in center field.

In 1961, Piersall finished third in batting in the American League with a .322 average. It would be the highest one-season average of his career. He also won his second Gold Glove that year.

Despite his fine showing, Piersall was traded to the Washington Senators. He spent a season and a half with the Senators before being dealt to the New York Mets.

Piersall didn't remain in New York for very long. But his brief career there was made memorable by an incident that took place on June 23, 1963. Piersall hit his one hundredth home run. He had promised to run the bases backward (but in the proper order) when he hit it. He kept his word. Because he had been practicing, he was able to travel at a good rate of speed. The fans loved it.

New York manager Casey Stengel didn't think the prank was funny. He released Piersall two days later. Piersall was hitting .194 at the time, which may have had something to do with the manager's decision.

Before the season was over, Piersall was picked up by the Los Angeles (now California) Angels. One afternoon when the Angels were playing the New York Yankees at Yankee Stadium, Piersall pulled one of his most laughable stunts. In the fifth inning, the Yankees bats exploded, and the team raked the Angels pitching for eight runs. Time after time, Piersall, in center field, had to chase down balls drilled to his left and right and over his head. He was worn out from all the running.

The bases were loaded when Angels manager Bill Rigney went to the mound to talk to the pitcher who had been the victim of the Yankees assault. After deciding to allow the pitcher to remain in the game, Rigney returned to the dugout.

Play was about to resume when the plate umpire suddenly whipped off his mask and shouted, "Time!" The ump had noticed that center field was vacant. Where was Piersall? A search was launched.

He was finally discovered hiding behind the granite monuments dedicated to Babe Ruth and Lou Gehrig in center field.

"Hey, I've got a wife and nine kids, and I've been chasing balls all afternoon," Piersall explained. "Someone's liable to get hurt out there. I'm not coming back until you get that guy off the mound."

Rigney shook his head in disbelief. Then the umpire told the Angels manager that he *had* to remove the pitcher. In the confusion, Rigney had gone to the mound a second time to speak to his pitcher. Because he had made two visits to the mound, he was required to make a pitching change. Satisfied, Piersall returned to center field.

Piersall stayed with the Angels as a part-time outfielder until he retired in 1967. After his retirement, Piersall continued to be a mischief maker. But he often brought harm to himself. As a baseball broadcaster for the Chicago White Sox, Piersall was fired from being too critical of the team. As a minor league instructor for the Chicago Cubs, he was let go for what team officials called "inappropriate conduct."

Late in the 1990s, Piersall seemed to find a job for which he was suited. He became the host of a sports-talk show for a Chicago radio station. The format allowed Piersall to spout and storm as much as he liked. Piersall was happy.

DRAWN OUT

Shea Stadium in New York, home of the Mets, has a reputation for zaniness. Crazy things often happen there.

Take the game between the Mets and the Astros on August 21, 1979. Play was in the top of the ninth inning. Two Astros had been retired. The Mets led, 5–0.

When outfielder Jeff Leonard flied out for the inning's third out, the Mets players sprinted from the field.

But then the plate umpire started waving his arms, signaling the Mets players to go back out onto the field. The game wasn't over. Frank Taveras, the Mets shortstop, had asked for a time-out just before the pitch, and the third base umpire had granted it. Leonard's turn at bat wasn't valid. He would have to return to the batter's box.

On his second attempt, Leonard lashed out a single. Then Mets manager Joe Torre protested. Ed Kranepool, the Mets first baseman, who, like his teammates had believed Leonard had been retired in his first at bat and that the game had ended, had left the field. But Kranepool had never returned to the playing field. Torre argued that game could not be started or restarted without nine men on the field. Thus, Leonard's base hit didn't count. The umpires agreed. Leonard's base hit was erased. He would have to bat again.

On his third try, Leonard flied out to left field. Now the game was really over. The Mets players breathed a sigh of relief and left the field.

But wait! The game had not ended. National League president Chub Feeney said that the umpires had made a mistake. He upheld a protest filed by the Astros. It claimed that time was not out simply because first baseman Kranepool did not happen to be on the field when Leonard got his base hit. That hit indeed counted.

The next day, the game was replayed from that point. There were two outs and Leonard was on first base.

José Cruz went to the plate for the Astros. He bounced out to second base for the final out. The game was finally over.

BLOWOUT

On the night of May 27, 1981, the Kansas City Royals faced the Seattle Mariners in a night game at Seattle's Kingdome. Batting in the top of the sixth inning, Kansas City's Amos Otis topped a ball toward third base. The Mariners catcher, shortstop, and third baseman each darted for the ball. The ball rolled slowly and no one tried to pick it up because there was little chance of throwing Otis out at first base.

The ball kept rolling, hugging the line. The Mariners only hope was that it would roll foul.

Suddenly, Mariners third baseman Lenny Randle dropped down on all fours. With his lips just inches from the ball, he started blowing at the ball. As Randle huffed and puffed, the ball began edging toward the foul line and finally it crossed into foul territory.

Randle jumped to his feet, a look of triumph on his face.

Umpire Larry McCoy signaled a foul ball. Amos Otis was called back from first base to continue his turn at bat.

With that, manager Jim Frey came bounding out of the Kansas City dugout to protest. He cited the rule that says a player can do nothing to alter the course of a baseball.

Umpire McCoy reversed his call. The ball was fair. Otis was credited with a base hit.

Afterward, Randle joked with reporters. "I didn't blow on it," he said. "I talked to the ball. I told it, 'Go foul! Go foul!'

"'The Bird' [Detroit pitcher Mark Fidrych] used to talk to the ball, and he didn't get into trouble.

"How could they call it a hit? It was a foul ball."

GREAT EXPECTATIONS

For years after the great Babe Ruth retired in 1935, the baseball world longed for someone with Ruthian qualities, an appealing and colorful performer who could hit the ball a mile. During the early 1940s, the Chicago Cubs believed they might have found such a player in Lou Novikoff, a broad-shouldered minor leaguer who had been a crowd favorite wherever he had played.

Novikoff had a notable career in the minors. In 1939 he was the leading hitter in the Texas League, with a .368 average. *The Sporting News* named him Minor League Player of the Year.

In 1940, Novikoff was even better. He batted .363 and hit forty home runs with the Los Angeles Angels of the Pacific Coast League. Such national magazines as *Esquire, The Saturday Evening Post, Look,* and *Collier's* hailed him for his awesome hitting.

The Chicago Cubs were impressed. The club purchased the twenty-five-year-old Novikoff from the Angels for $100,000, a record price at the time.

Novikoff, whose parents had been born in Russia, was nicknamed "The Mad Russian." In Novikoff's case, as the Cubs soon realized, the word mad didn't mean angry; it meant crazy.

Novikoff's screwball qualities first became apparent in the outfield. In Wrigley Field, the Chicago team's home park, Novikoff would back up only so far and no farther on fly balls hit toward him. As a result, balls were always soaring over his head and bouncing off the wall.

Cubs manager Charlie Grimm demanded an explanation. Novikoff claimed that he had a terrible fear of vines. Yes, *vines*! He was terrified that one would touch him. Since the outfield at Wrigley Field was vine covered, this made for a real problem.

Grimm tried to convince Novikoff that the vines were harmless. He rubbed vine leaves and stems on his hands and face. He even chewed vine pieces. But nothing that Grimm did could cure Novikoff's fear. Long drives to the outfield kept sailing over his head.

Novikoff also proved to be a wacko on the base paths. He once tried to steal third with the bases loaded. When he came back to the bench, he was met by a furious Grimm.

"How could you do a dumb thing like that?" Grimm wanted to know.

Novikoff was serene. "I had such a good jump on the pitcher," he said, "that I just couldn't resist."

Novikoff's failings might have been overlooked if he had lived up to his billing as a slugger. But he did not. Home runs were a rarity for him. He hit only five during his rookie season of 1941.

Once, when Novikoff was having a particularly bad day at the plate, Grimm took him out of the game. "I know why they call you the Mad Russian," Grimm said to him. "If I couldn't hit any better than you, I'd be mad, too."

In 1942, Novikoff hit .300 for the season. He averaged .279 in 1943 and .281 in 1944. But Novikoff's many flaws as a fielder and base runner often wiped out his value as a hitter.

The Cubs dealt Novikoff to the Phillies in 1944. After seventeen games with the Philadelphia team, he was back in the minor leagues. He played with an assortment of teams until he retired in 1951.

NICE CATCH

On August 21, 1908, twenty-six-year-old Charles "Gabby" Street, a catcher for the Washington Senators, won instant and long-lasting fame for pulling off a truly daring stunt. To win a $500 bet, the chatty Street caught a baseball dropped from near the top of the Washington Monument.

The Washington Monument, a tapering shaft of white marble, is 555 feet, 5 1/8 inches (169 meters) in height. But the ball Street caught didn't travel that distance. It was tossed out of one of the eight small windows, two on each side, that are located at the monument's 500-foot level.

Catching a ball from 500 feet was no easy matter. It took five seconds for the ball to reach Street. In the last second, the ball fell 140 feet (43 meters), according to *The New York Times*. That means that it was traveling faster than a good fastball.

The day was windy, which made the feat much more difficult. Street missed thirteen tosses before he was able to snag and hold one.

When the plummeting ball got close, Street reached up for it. It struck his mitt with a loud whack that could be heard, said the *Times*, "several hundred yards away."

Although Street rubbed his hands afterward, the stunt didn't seem to cause him any pain or suffering. That afternoon he was in his customary position behind home plate when the Senators played the Detroit Tigers.

POWERLESS

In 1973 the American League adopted the designated hitter rule. It states: "A hitter may be designated to bat for the starting pitcher and all subsequent pitchers in any game. . . ." In other words, the hitter does not have to play in the field.

The rule is still in effect, of course. It is meant to boost the American League's offensive punch by doing away with plate appearances by weak-hitting pitchers. Johnny Broaca is a case in point.

Broaca, a right-hander who pitched for several years for the New York Yankees beginning in 1934, hated to bat. A trip to the plate was sheer torture for him. When his turn arrived, he would take his stance with his bat on his shoulder and simply wait for the pitcher to pour the ball past him three times. Silent and grim-faced, he'd then trudge back to the dugout.

On days that he was scheduled to pitch, Broaca refused to take batting practice. Why bother, he figured. He was only going to stand at the plate like a statue. He stayed in a corner of the clubhouse until batting practice had ended.

Broaca's first hit as a major leaguer was accidental. In a game against the Washington Senators, Broaca took his familiar stance at the plate, his bat resting on his right shoulder. The pitcher's throw was wild and it went behind Broaca, striking his bat and caroming over the third baseman's head.

In another game during his rookie season, Broaca batted five times and struck out five times. For Broaca, that was his version of a perfect day at the plate.

Broaca went from the Yankees to the Indians in 1939, and ended his career with the Cleveland team. As a pitcher he had a decent career. He won fifteen games in 1935. He twice won twelve games.

But as a hitter he was a total flop. He went to bat 254 times. He collected twenty-three hits, or less than five hits a season. His lifetime batting average was .091. That kind of showing helped hasten the day of the designated hitter.

FUMBLE KING

Dick Stuart's nicknames tipped off the kind of fielder he was. A first baseman with the Pittsburgh Pirates for five seasons beginning in 1958, and for several other teams in the five seasons that followed, Stuart was known as "Dr. Strangeglove" for the freakish things the ball often did once it came in contact with his mitt. "Stonefingers" was another of his nicknames.

Sometimes Stuart was referred to as "Clank." That was the sound the ball was said to make when it went caroming off of his fingers.

There's plenty of statistical evidence to support the idea that Stuart was no Lou Gehrig. From 1958 through 1964, Stuart led the major leagues, or tied for the lead, in the number of errors in a season for a first baseman.

Pittsburgh fans regularly booed Stuart for his miscues. But one night he earned their cheers. A hot dog wrapper came floating out of the stands and drifted toward first base. Stuart caught it on the fly. Some 30,000 fans gave him a standing ovation.

Stuart shrugged off the criticism he got for his poor fielding. In fact, he seemed to enjoy the attention it brought him. One year he ordered a license plate that read "E-3"—the scoring symbol for "Error, first baseman."

Fielding wasn't Stuart's only frailty. He also left a great deal to be desired as a base runner. He was always misreading or completely missing the coach's signs. He once suggested, "When I get on, why not just point to the base you want me to go to."

Stuart's great virtue was that he had exceptional power. He could win a ballgame with one swing of his bat.

"I know I'm the world's worst fielder," he said. "But who gets paid for fielding? There isn't one great fielder in baseball getting the kind of dough that I get paid for hitting."

As a power hitter, Stuart's best season came in 1963 after he had been traded to the Boston Red Sox. He had 42 home runs and a league high of 118 runs batted in. He earned Comeback Player of Year honors that season. But Boston fans booed him for his twenty-nine errors.

By 1967, Stuart was playing in Japan. He was unhappy there and stayed only one season. In 1969, after playing first base and pinch-hitting for the California Angels in twenty-two games, Stuart retired.

Unfortunately for Dick Stuart, he played before the introduction of the designated hitter. If Stuart never had to pick up a glove and just hit, his career might have lasted many more years, even decades more perhaps.

THE GREATEST

If baseball's record keepers had a category for "Heaviest Players, Career," Walter "Jumbo" Brown would be at the top of the list. A pitcher who performed in both the American and National leagues for a decade and a half beginning in 1925, Brown weighed an awesome 298 pounds (135 kilograms).

Brown weighed a mere 197 pounds (89 kilograms) when he joined the Cleveland Indians in 1927. Since that weight was spread over a 6-foot 4-inch (193-centimeter) frame, Brown appeared merely big, not beefy.

At the end of the season, Brown had his tonsils removed. Afterward, he began to enjoy eating as never before. When he showed up at spring training the next year, he had gotten so large that his teammates hardly recognized him.

By 1929, Jumbo was back in the minor leagues, where he toiled for four years. The Yankees invited Jumbo to spring training in 1932. A New York sportswriter noted that Jumbo "weighed two pounds more than an elephant." He had to work out in a T-shirt because the club didn't have a uniform jersey big enough to fit him.

Jumbo had the best season of his career in 1933, winning seven games. He made headlines that year by talking some of his teammates into playing a game of leapfrog. When it became Jumbo's turn to do the leaping, his teammates crumpled under his weight. Outfielder Sam Bryant and infielder Cy Perkins ended up on the injury list.

Despite his clownishness, Jumbo stayed with the Yankees for four seasons. New York fans joked that he looked like "the man who swallowed a taxicab."

When he retired in 1941, he had won a total of thirty-three games, not exactly a Hall of Fame career. Jumbo is remembered not so much for tossing fastballs and curves but, as sportswriter Bruce Nash once noted, "for throwing the biggest shadow in baseball."

SPACEMAN

"If I were commissioner of baseball, I'd get rid of the designated hitter and artificial turf. I'd maintain smaller ballparks and revamp quality old ballparks. I'd outlaw instant video replays. I'd outlaw mascots. I'd put organic food in the stands. I would bring back warm, roasted peanuts. Just the smell of grass and those warm, roasted peanuts should be enough to make people come to the park."

That's Bill Lee talking. During his fourteen-years as a fine control pitcher for the Boston Red Sox and Montreal Expos, the colorful Lee would speak his mind on almost any subject. He was always being quoted.

From 1969 through 1982, Lee won 119 games, lost 90, and compiled a 3.62 earned run average. He won 17 games in 1973, 1974, and 1975. His career included an All-Star appearance in 1973 and two starts in the 1975 World Series.

But Lee earned more headlines with his lip than his assortment of junkballs. When he joined the Red Sox in 1969 and got his first look at the "Green Monster," the towering left-field wall at Fenway Park that intrudes upon the playing field, he was asked what he thought of it.

"Do they leave it there during games?" he asked.

He once described Boston's beloved slugger Carl Yastrzemski as a "dull and boring potato farmer from Long Island who just happened to be a great ballplayer." He also called Yaz "the worst dresser in baseball . . . he had the same London Fog raincoat during his entire career. We'd throw it in trash cans all around the league and somehow it always made its way back."

Another time Lee was asked, "When you pitch, what do you most often think about?"

"I most often think about not trying to think," Lee said. "Thinking only gets you in trouble."

Of the weak-hitting California Angels, Lee once said, "They could take batting practice in the Grand Hotel and not bother a chandelier."

After the Red Sox lost game two of the 1975 World Series, a reporter, looking for an insightful comment, asked Lee, "How would you characterize the series so far?"

Lee looked thoughtful for a moment, then replied: "Tied."

During the series, umpire Larry Barnett failed to make an inter-ference ruling against Ed Armbrister at home plate. The lapse may have cost the Red Sox the game. Lee felt that the Boston manager had not argued with enough enthusiasm. "I'd have bitten Barnett's ear off," Lee said.

Lee had stormy relations with Don Zimmer, another of his Red Sox managers. He led a revolt against the stumpy Zimmer, whom he called "the gerbil." (Lee thought the manager looked like the small rodent.)

Lee was known as "The Spaceman" during his career. He got the nickname after a 1969 radio interview. Instead of baseball, Lee insisted on discussing the first lunar landing, which had taken place that year.

On the mound, Lee was never still, roaming from side to side and back and forth. He would sometimes field ground balls behind his back or between his legs. One year, Lee introduced a pitch that he called the moonball. It traveled lazily in a rainbow-shaped arc. Tony Perez of the Reds hit a two-run homer off the pitch in the sixth inning of the seventh game of the 1975 World Series. At the time, Lee was seeking to protect a 3–0 lead. Perez's home run revived the sagging Cincinnati team, and they won, 4–3. Lee put the moonball in mothballs after that.

The following season, Lee took part in a wild bench-clearing brawl at Yankee Stadium in New York that cost him heavily. When the hostilities ended, Lee tottered from the field clutching has left arm. At the hospital he learned that he had ripped ligaments in the shoulder. He was put on the disabled list.

After the injury, Lee never had another winning season with the Red Sox. Dealt to the Montreal Expos, he regained his form in 1979, winning sixteen games.

Lee's career came to an abrupt end in 1982 after the Expos released light-hitting infielder Rodney Scott, a close friend of Lee's. Lee screamed in protest, saying that the club shouldn't do such a thing to such a nice guy. He stormed out of the ballpark to show his displeasure.

The Expos were quick to react, fining Lee $5,000 and releasing him. Afterward, Lee telephoned several National League clubs to inquire about employment. None showed any interest.

That didn't stop Lee. From his home in Craftsbury, Vermont, Lee began touring with a group of big-league old-timers, playing exhibition games throughout much of North America and Cuba, too. "There's a lot more baseball than the major leagues," he said.

In the summer of 2000, Lee, at age fifty-three, was still playing baseball and was still a popular figure. And he was still being quoted, telling an interviewer from *Sports Illustrated* how he would strike out Cardinals home-run hero Mark McGwire. "I'd run him nothing but fastballs up and in," Lee said, "then a straight change away, and Good Night, Irene!"

GOOF-OFFS

Major leaguers know how to concentrate. On every pitch, infielders and outfielders are totally focused, looking in toward home plate, ready to react. Mental lapses are rare. When one does occur, however, most people in the ballpark know it, and sometimes the guilty party gets branded for life for his slipup.

Take what happened in a game at New York's Shea Stadium in 1980. The Mets were playing the Los Angeles Dodgers. In the seventh inning, with the Mets leading, 6–5, Ron Cey, the Dodgers third baseman, came to bat. Steve Garvey was at first base for the Dodgers.

Cey worked the count to 2-and-2. In came the next pitch. Cey looked it over, decided it was a ball, tossed his bat away, and headed for first base. The pitch was a ball, but it wasn't ball four, of course; it was only ball three.

When Steve Garvey saw Cey trotting down the first baseline, he figured that his teammate knew what he was doing. Garvey turned and started for second base.

The confused Dodgers base runners didn't influence Mets catcher John Stearns. He knew that the count was actually 3-and-2. He knew that Garvey and Cey weren't paying attention. Stearns fired the ball to second and easily nabbed Garvey.

When Cey saw the play at second, he suddenly realized that he had goofed. His chin was on his chest as he returned to home plate to resume his turn at bat. The Dodgers never recovered from the base-running blunders, and lost.

A similar incident had taken place two years earlier, in 1978, in a game in Philadelphia between the Phillies and the Mets. But on this occasion the umpires and an entire team became daydreamy.

It was the ninth inning. The Phillies led, 9–4. Tug McGraw was pitching for the Philadelphia team. Lenny Randle came to the plate for the Mets. The count reached 3-and-2. McGraw's next pitch was a high and outside fastball—ball four.

But Randle miscounted. He didn't realize that the count was ball four and that he had been issued a base on balls. He somehow had the idea that it was only ball three.

Randle stepped out of the batter's box, reached down and got some dirt, and rubbed his hands together. Then he marched up to the plate again to face McGraw.

It seemed like almost everyone in the ballpark was influenced by Randle. The confused scoreboard operator certainly was. He allowed the count to remain at 3-and-2.

Home plate umpire John Kibbler was probably misled by the scoreboard. He allowed Randle to remain at the plate instead of directing him to first base. The other umpires were led astray by chief umpire Kibbler.

Tug McGraw was one of the few people who knew what was taking place. He realized that he had thrown ball four, and that several of the Mets and the umpires were asleep. He could hardly wait to get the ball back from the catcher so he could deliver another pitch.

McGraw should have been less anxious. When he did pitch to Randle, the New York infielder slammed the ball into left field for a triple. McGraw then settled down and retired the next three batters, stranding Randle at third.

The mass forgetfulness on the part of the Mets played no part in the game's outcome. The Phillies were easy winners. But the incident did establish what might have been the only instance in baseball history where a batter got to swing at a 4-and-2 pitch.

YOUNGSTER

Early in World War II (1941–1945), President Franklin D. Roosevelt gave major league baseball the "green light" to continue play. It was decided that games would be useful entertainment for the nation in general and war workers in particular.

But during the war years, teams were faced with a critical shortage of players. Physically fit adult males had been called into the armed services. To make do, clubs signed players who were unacceptable to the military. Some of these rejects were too old; others, too young.

Joe Nuxhall was one of those chosen because of his youthfulness. A promising schoolboy pitcher, Nuxhall was fifteen years old when he joined the Cincinnati Reds in 1944. He was in ninth grade. He had to get permission from his school principal to sign with the team.

During the early weeks of the season, when school was still in session, Nuxhall was allowed to be with the team only on weekends and occasionally for a night game. But once summer vacation began, he joined the team on a full-time basis.

One June afternoon at Crosley Field, the St. Louis Cardinals pounded the Reds, building a 13–0 lead. The Cards were the National League's most fearsome team. They had captured the pennant in 1943 and were to be World Series winners in 1944.

Nuxhall and his teammates watched silently from the dugout as the Cardinals lashed out one hit after another. Suddenly, Nuxhall heard his name being called by manager Bill McKechnie. "Joe, go to the bullpen and warm up," McKechnie said. Nuxhall could hardly believe his ears. He had seen only a handful of major league games. He had not pitched. He had no idea he would be called upon so soon.

The date was June 10, 1944. Joe was about to make history. At the time, he was fifteen years, ten months, and eleven days old. He was about to become the youngest player ever to play for a major-league team.

It would be nice to be able to say that Joe Nuxhall's debut was a success, that he bewildered the St. Louis hitters with fastballs and curves. It didn't happen. Nuxhall's first appearance as a major leaguer was an embarrassment.

After manager McKechnie had summoned him, Joe tripped on the dugout steps as he headed for the bullpen. He landed on his face.

When he was called into the game, his heart was pounding. The last time he had pitched was against high school kids. He couldn't control his warm-up throws, several of which eluded the catcher.

Once the pitches counted, Nuxhall walked two hitters and retired two. Then Stan Musial came to the plate. Musial was in the early stages of his legendary career with the St. Louis team. The year before, he had been the league's hitting champion. Nuxhall came apart. He gave up five runs on two hits and five walks before McKechnie took him out of the game.

Within forty-eight hours, Nuxhall was assigned to a Cincinnati farm team in Birmingham, Alabama.

That was not the end of Joe Nuxhall, however. He battled back. He pitched for seven years in the minor leagues to win a second chance with the Reds, returning to the team in 1952. In the seasons that followed, he became a fixture with the Reds. Nuxhall was a seventeen-game winner in 1955. When he retired in 1966, he had compiled a 135-117 won-lost record.

There's more. Nuxhall went on to become a Reds broadcaster. That career lasted for more than thirty years.

By the time Nuxhall began thinking of retiring as a broadcaster, he had spent seven decades in baseball. Few people in Cincinnati could remember very much about Nuxhall's sixteen-year career as a pitcher for the Reds. Fewer still could recall his ill-fated introduction to the game.

DAFFY DODGERS

The Brooklyn Dodgers of the 1920s featured a great array of block-heads, players who were known more for their foolish or even stupid on-the-field antics than anything else. "The Daffiness Boys" they were called.

Take what happened at Ebbets Field in Brooklyn on the afternoon of August 15, 1926. The Dodgers were playing the Boston Braves. The score was tied, 1–1, with one out in the seventh inning.

Chick Fewster, an infielder, was the runner at first base. Dazzy Vance, the Brooklyn pitcher, was on second. Hank DeBerry, Vance's catcher, was at third. Outfielder Babe Herman, one of the team's more clownish figures, stepped up to the plate to face Boston pitcher George Mogridge, a leftie. Mogridge delivered and Herman swung, driving the ball to right field. The Boston outfielder moved to make the catch, but the ball sailed over his head and caromed off the fence. DeBerry trotted across home plate with the tie-breaking run.

Vance hesitated for a second, then raced for third and rounded the base, getting halfway to the plate. Fewster also held up briefly before rounding second and setting out for third. As Fewster neared third, Herman, head down and running at full tilt, was right behind him.

Mickey O'Neil, the Dodger third base coach, could see a disaster coming. "Back! Back!" he shouted to Herman, meaning the Babe should return to second base.

But Dazzy Vance, midway between third and home, thought that O'Neil was yelling at him. Vance instantly reversed course, retreating back to third. He slid in at about the same time Fewster was executing his slide into the base.

Herman paid no attention to O'Neil's cry of alarm. He went into third, too, joining Fewster and Vance. The Dodgers had accomplished what may have been a baseball first—three runners all on third base.

Eddie Taylor, the Boston third baseman, got the ball and tagged all three men. Vance, as the lead runner, was entitled to third base. But Herman and Fewster were called out. What Herman had done was double into a double play.

The era of the Daffiness Boys lasted into the 1930s. Herman was traded to the Cincinnati Reds in 1932. He retired in 1937. But during World War II, when major league baseball experienced a player shortage, the Dodgers brought back the Babe.

He was forty-two. In his first game in almost a decade, he was called upon as a pinch hitter and lashed out a single. The crowd roared in delight. But then, in timeless fashion, the Babe tripped over first base.

FREE SPIRIT

A stereotype, says the dictionary, is the popular image that society has established for a person or a group. One stereotype is that people who wear glasses are smart. Like most stereotypes, this one doesn't always jibe with the facts.

There's a baseball stereotype that applies to left-handed pitchers. It says that southpaws are the zaniest of the zany, true flakes. As Exhibit A, consider Yankee pitcher Vernon "Lefty" Gomez, who was nicknamed "Goofy." He once announced his plans to build a "fish saver." It was to take the form of a revolving goldfish bowl. Its residents would never have to swim.

Then there's Will McEnaney, a lefty pitcher with the Montreal Expos. As a minor leaguer, McEnaney liked to walk an imaginary dog outside the clubhouse.

For another real oddball among lefties, baseball historians often cite George Edward "Rube" Waddell, a stocky 6 footer with a fearsome overhand delivery. Waddell's plaque in the Hall of Fame refers to him as a "colorful left-handed pitcher." "Colorful" isn't strong enough.

Waddell wrestled alligators and jumped out of hotel windows. He would disappear from the team for days at a time. On game days, he would race out of the ballpark to pursue passing fire engines. He was sometimes late for games because he was playing marbles with neighborhood kids.

Rube's onetime manager, the legendary Connie Mack of the Philadelphia A's, once said of him: "The Rube has a two million dollar body and a two cent brain."

By the time he was eighteen, Waddell was already a star with a semipro team in Butler, Pennsylvania. The Louisville Colonels, then a National League team, paid him $500 to sign a contract. But Rube pitched only two games for the team before he packed up and left, unhappy with the manager's rules of discipline.

He moved on to Detroit in the Western League. In 1899 he won twenty-seven games with Columbus-Grand Rapids, also a Western League club.

Then Rube tried Louisville a second time. When the baseball season ended, Rube went to work as an alligator wrestler in Florida.

Rube pitched briefly for the Pittsburgh Pirates and Chicago Cubs before joining the Philadelphia Athletics, where he was to enjoy his best seasons. As manager and owner of the A's, Connie Mack learned to control Rube better than anyone else. Mack never gave Waddell his weekly salary all at once. He knew it would be gone in a heartbeat. Instead, he paid Rube only $10 or $15 at a time.

Mack also provided Rube with special incentives. Once, after Waddell had just finished pitching a seventeen-inning game, Mack made him an offer. Mack and the opposing manager had agreed to limit the second game of the day's doubleheader to five innings.

Before the game, Mack spoke to Waddell. "You can take off and go fishing for the next three days," he said, "if you'll pitch the second game." Rube threw a shutout.

Under Mack, Waddell earned a reputation as one of baseball's great strikeout artists. Every year from 1902 through 1907, he led the league in strikeouts. On July 2, 1902, he became the first pitcher to strike out the side on nine pitches. In 1904 he struck out 349 batters, setting baseball's all-time record. It lasted sixty-one years.

Players on opposing teams tried to figure out ways to beat Waddell. A pitcher for the St. Louis Browns had an idea. He would try to get Rube's arm weary before a game, hoping to reduce his effectiveness.

"I know you can throw the ball hard," the pitcher said to Rube before the game. "But I can throw farther than you can."

Rube laughed at the man.

"I'll *bet* I can," said the pitcher. Rube agreed to a small wager.

The two men marched out to deep center field. They would throw toward home plate. The man who threw the greatest distance would win.

The St. Louis pitcher threw first. The ball traveled as far as second base before rolling to a stop. Then Rube threw. The ball skidded off the infield dirt and kept going, ending up well behind home plate.

The St. Louis pitcher was not surprised. He knew that he was overmatched. But his mind was working.

"Let's make it four out of seven," he said.

Rube shrugged. He put his next three throws beyond home plate. His opponent's tosses barely made it to the infield.

The St. Louis pitcher pretended to be surprised. "That's amazing!" he said. "Can you do that again?" Rube was flattered. He was happy to keep demonstrating his power.

When the session ended, the pitcher handed over the money to Rube. Both players went to their dugouts to await the start of the game. The St. Louis pitcher laughed to himself, certain he would be facing an opponent with a worn-out arm.

But that afternoon, Rube was his usual self, virtually unhittable. He struck out fourteen batters, cruising to an easy win.

After the game, Rube happened to run into the St. Louis pitcher who had tried to trick him. "Hey, thanks for the workout," Rube said. "That was swell practice."

Once, after a very successful year, Rube told Connie Mack that he wouldn't sign his contract for the season to come. Mack was not pleased. He felt he had been generous in his dealings with the left-hander. He granted him days off to go fishing. He had permitted him to visit firehouses when the team was on the road. He stood ready to provide the money that Rube might need to get out of any troublesome situations that might arise. What else did Rube want?

Rube explained that his problem involved his catcher and close buddy, Ossee Schreckengost. He and Rube roomed together when the team traveled. In those days, pairs of players not only roomed together but they also often shared the same bed. Waddell had no objection in splitting a mattress with Schreckengost. What bothered him was Schreckengost's habit of eating crackers in bed. That had to be stopped.

Mack was sympathetic. He had a clause written into Schreckengost's contract that put an end to the cracker munching.

That made Rube happy. He signed for the season.

When the A's captured the American League pennant in 1905, Waddell was the ace of the team's pitching staff. He won twenty-seven games and lost only ten.

When the A's played in the World Series, Waddell was a spectator. During the last weeks of the season, he and teammate Andy Coakley

had gotten into a scuffle. Coakley fell on Waddell's left arm, injuring it. Waddell was unable to pitch in the series.

Connie Mack eventually sold Waddell to the St. Louis Browns. In his first appearance for the Browns, Waddell set a single-game record by striking out sixteen batters.

The Browns figured out a way of keeping Waddell out of trouble during the off-season. The club hired him to go hunting, something that he loved to do. Each week, Rube would head out into the woodlands in quest of duck, rabbit, deer, and other game. On Saturday, he'd show up at the Browns office for his salary. He was paid an amount that was meant to last him through the week, and never more than that.

After Waddell won only three games in 1910, St. Louis released him. He then pitched for Minneapolis in the American Association for three years. He died in 1914 while under treatment for a lung disease. He was thirty-eight.

Rube Waddell set about every pitching record there was. He ranks as one of the greatest left-handers in baseball history.

Strong-armed pitchers are always welcome in baseball, despite their reputation for daffiness. But no team today would put up with a pitcher who was also a fire-truck chaser, obsessed fisherman, marbles player, and alligator wrestler. Baseball characters like Rube Waddell are of the past.

INDEX

64

ABOUT THE AUTHOR

George Sullivan is the author of more than a hundred books for children and young adults, many of which have received awards or commendation. He also contributes to leading magazines. *Baseball's Boneheads, Bad Boys, and Just Plain Crazy Guys* is Sullivan's sixth book for The Millbrook Press. His other titles are: *Any Number Can Play: The Numbers Athletes Wear; Burnin' Rubber: Behind the Scenes in Stock Car Racing; The Civil War at Sea; Don't Step on the Foul Line: Sports Superstitions;* and *To the Bottom of the Sea: The Exploration of Exotic Life, the Titanic, and Other Secrets of the Oceans.* Sullivan lives in New York City and Key West with his wife Midge.